MY FIRST BOOK SLOVENIA

ALL ABOUT SLOVENIA FOR KIDS

GLOBED
CHILDREN BOOKS

Copyright 2023 by Globed Children Books

All rights reserved. No part of this book may be reproduced or distributed in any form without prior written permission from the author, with the exception of non-commercial uses permitted by copyright law.

Limited of Liability/Disclaimer of Warranty: The publisher and author make no representations or liabilities with respect to the accuracy and completeness of the contents of this work and specifically disclaim all warranties including without limitations warranties of fitness of particular purpose. No warranty may be created or extended by sales or promotional materials. This work is sold with the understanding that the publisher and author is not engaging in rendering medical, legal or any other professional advice or service. Further, readers should be aware that websites listed in this work may have changed or disappeared between when this work was written and when it is read.

Interior and cover Design: Daniel Day
Editor: Margaret Bam

For My Sons, Daniel, David and Jude

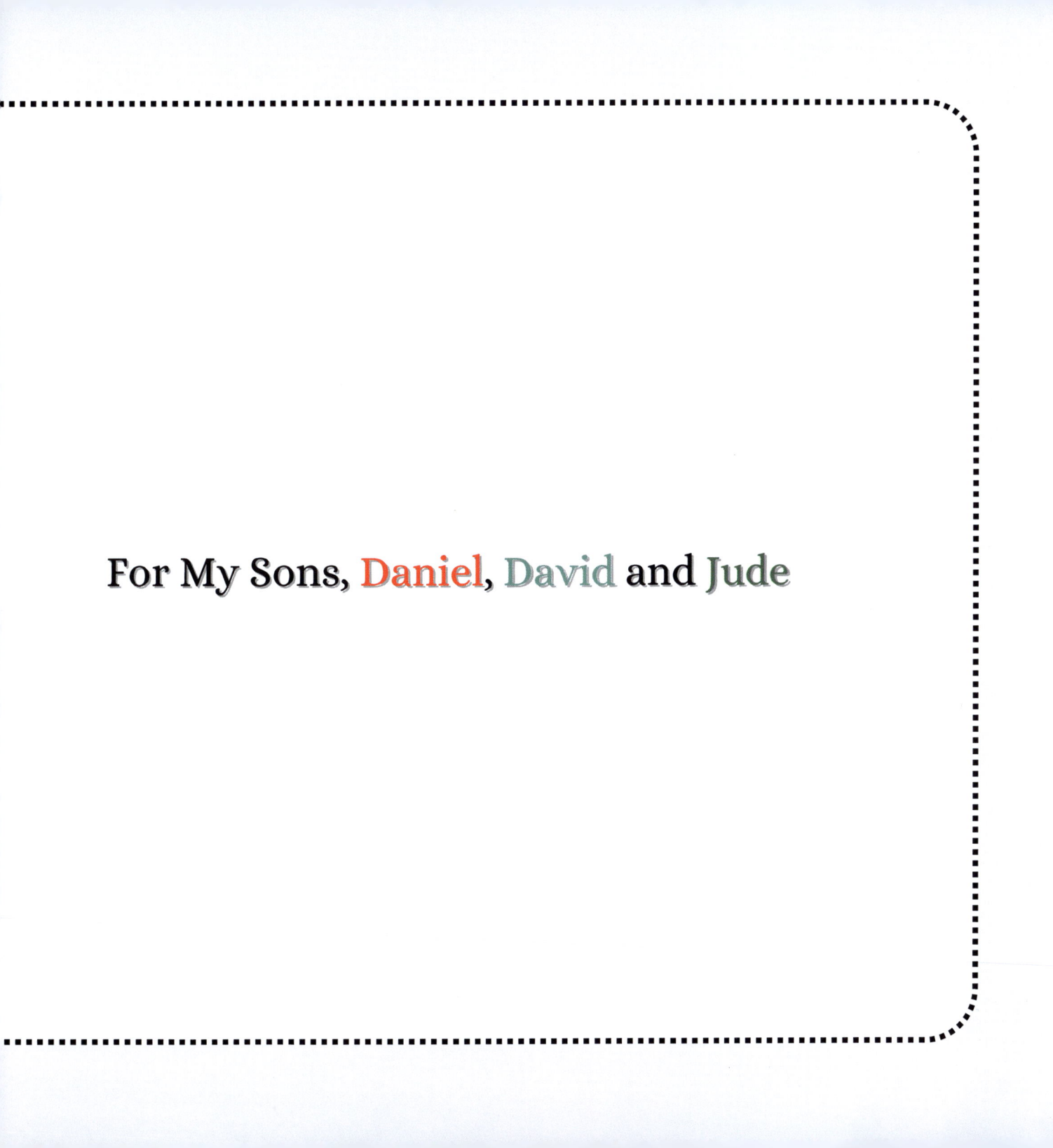

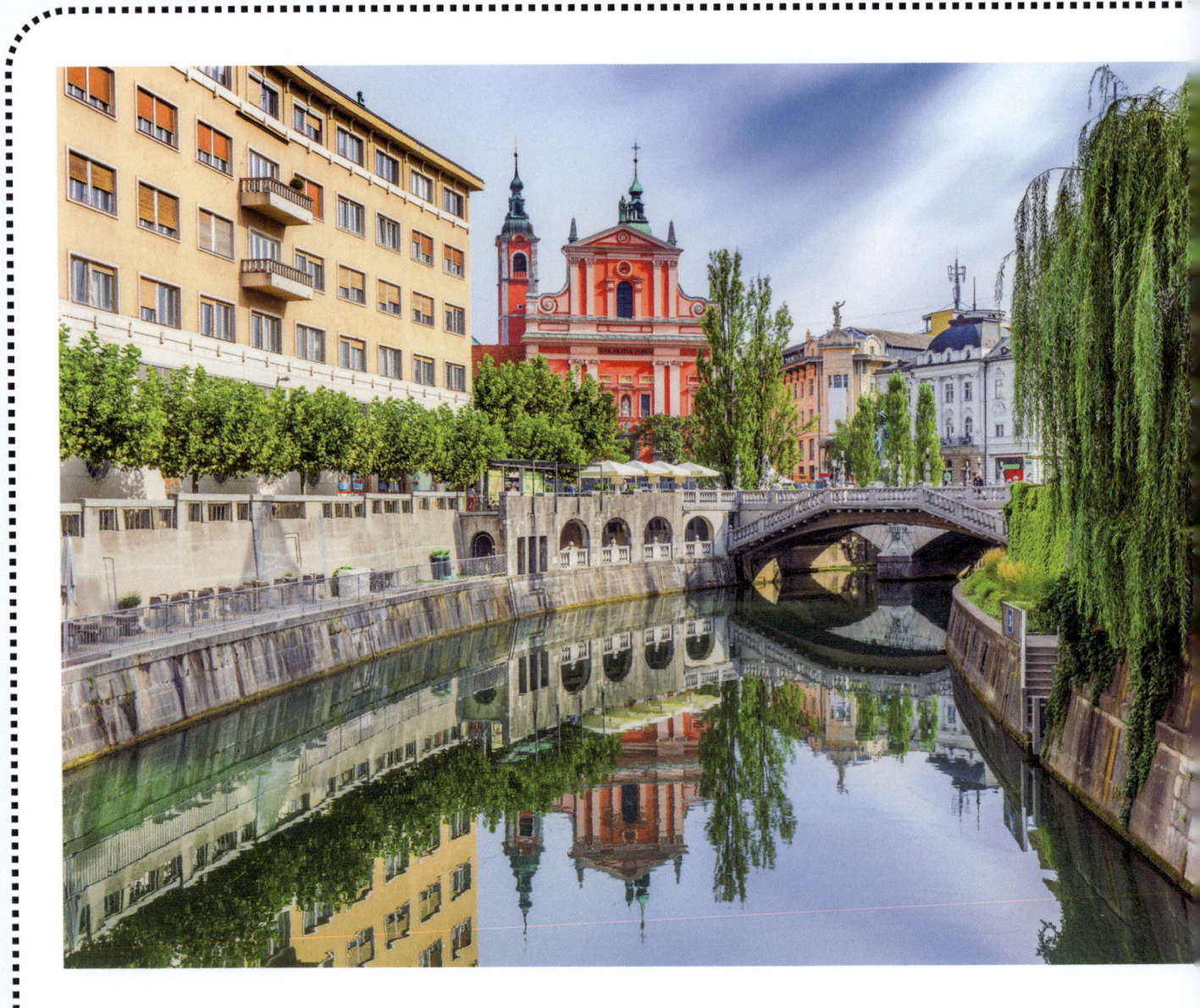

Ljubljana, Slovenia

Slovenia

Slovenia is a **country**.

A country is land that is controlled by a **single government**. Countries are also called **nations, states, or nation-states**.

Countries can be **different sizes**. Some countries are big and others are small.

Lake Bled, Slovenia

Where Is Slovenia?

Slovenia is located in the continent of **Europe.**

A continent is **a massive area of land that is separated from others by water or other natural features.**

Slovenia is situated in the central part of Europe.

Dragon statue and cathedral in Ljubljana, Slovenia

Capital

The capital of Slovenia is Ljubljana.

Ljubljana is located in the **central part** of the country.

Ljubljana is the largest city in Slovenia.

Ljubljana, Slovenia

Regions

Slovenia is a country that is made up of 12 regions

The regions of Slovenia are as follows:

Pomurska, Podravska, Koroška, Savinjska, Zasavska, Spodnjeposavska, Jugovzhodna Slovenija, Osrednjeslovenska, Gorenjska, Notranjsko-kraška, Goriška and Obalno-kraška.

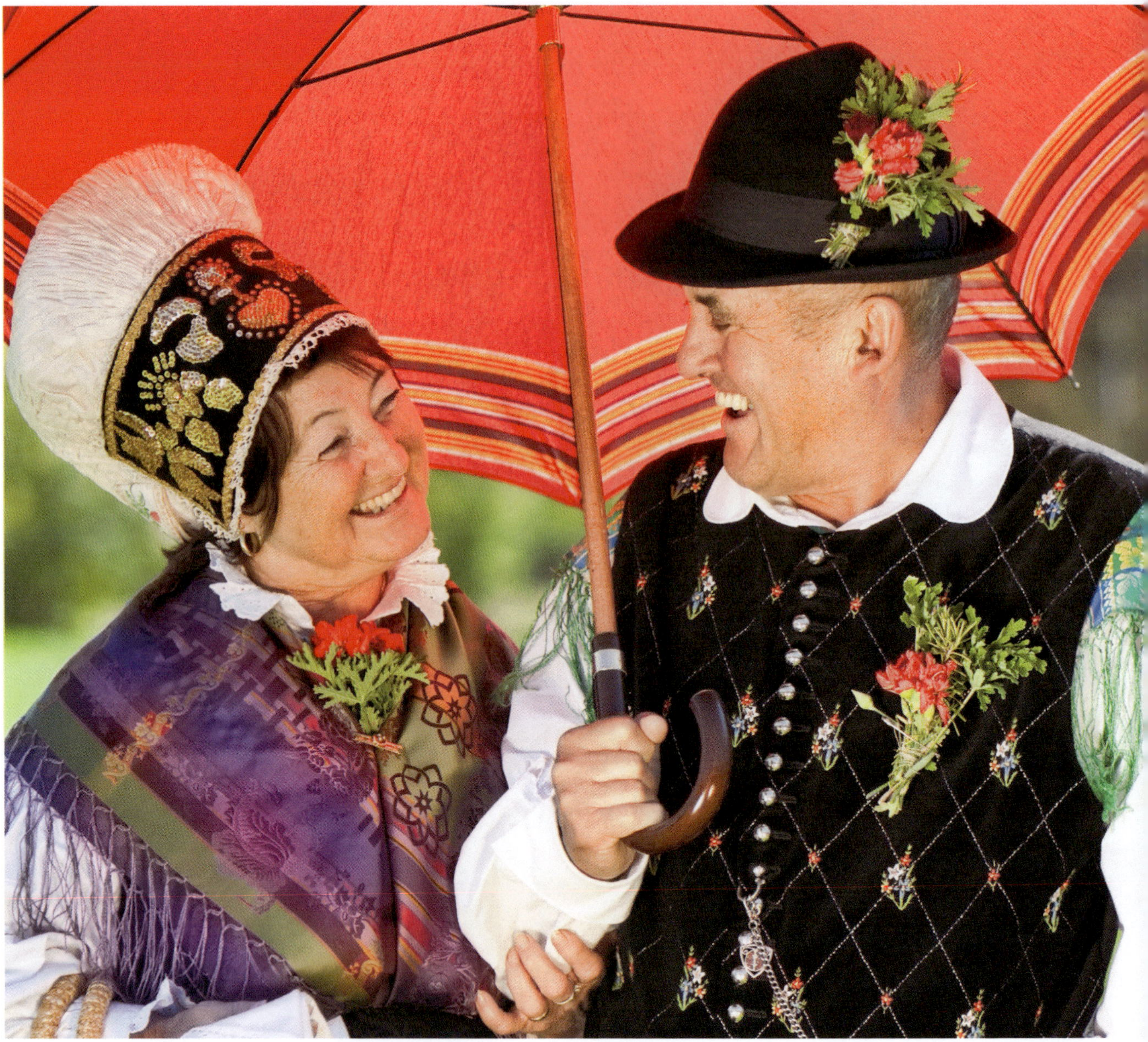

Population

Slovenia has population of around **2 million people** making it the 147th most populated country in the world and the 33rd most populated country in Europe.

Mountain pastures in Julian Alps, Slovenia

Size

Slovenia is **20,271 square kilometres** making it the 38th largest country in Europe by area.

Slovenia is the 150th largest country in the world.

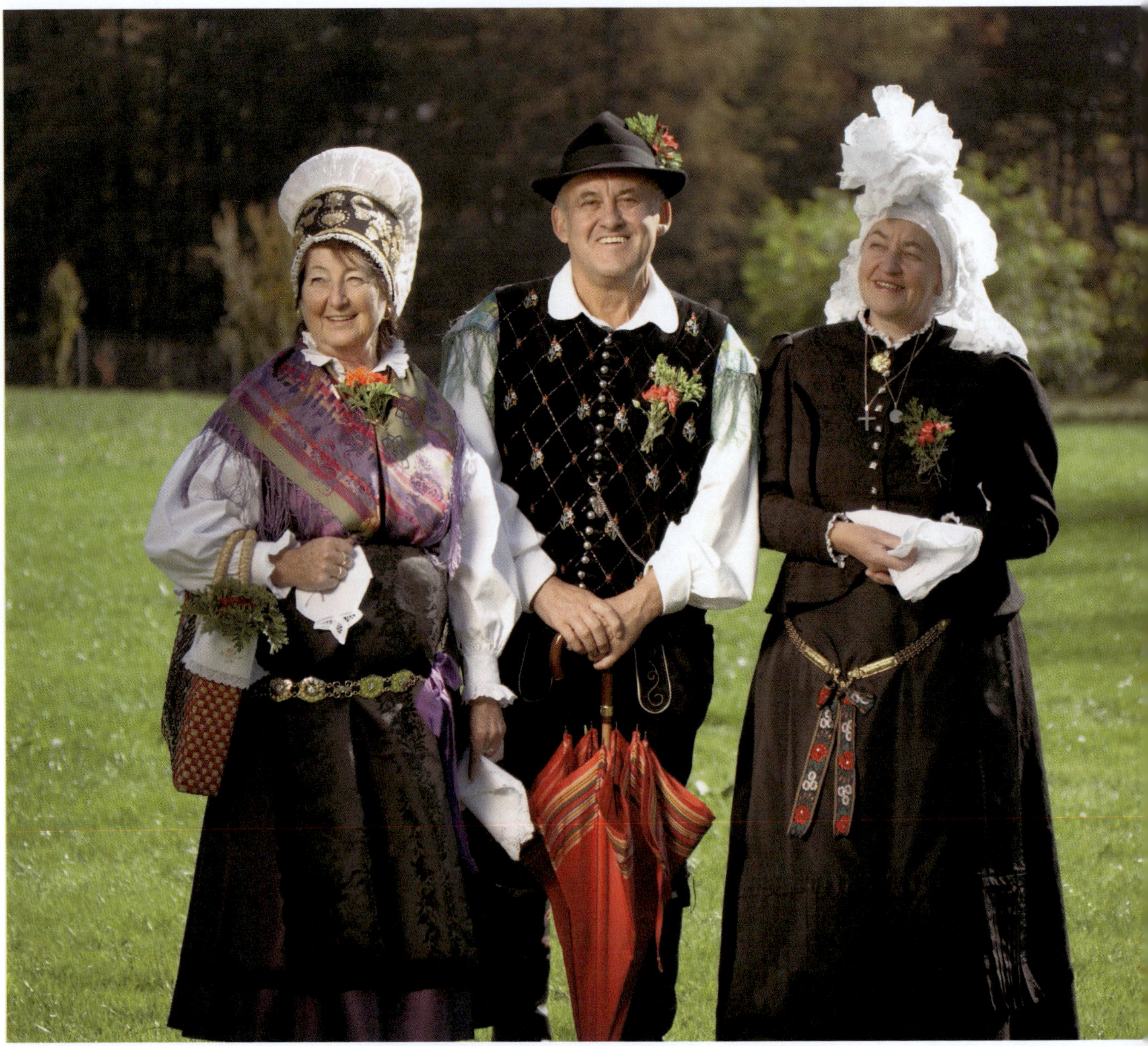

Languages

The official language of Slovenia is **Slovene**. The Slovene language is a Slavic language and is spoken by the majority of the population in Slovenia. Slovene is also recognized as a minority language in Austria, Hungary, Italy, and Croatia.

Italian and Hungarian are also spoken in Slovenia.

Here are a few Slovene phrases
- **Kako si? -** How are you?
- **Dobro jutro -** Good morning

Postojna Caves, Slovenia

Attractions

There are lots of interesting places to see in Slovenia.

Some beautiful places to visit in Slovenia are

- **Postojna Cave**
- **Soteska Vintgar**
- **Predjama Castle**
- **Tivoli Park**
- **Skocjan Caves**
- **Bled Castle**

Predjama Castle, Slovenia

History of Slovenia

People have lived in Slovenia for a very long time, the territory that is now known as Slovenia was first settled by Slavic tribes in the 6th century.

Slovenia came under the rule of the Frankish Empire in the 8th century, and later became part of the Holy Roman Empire.

After World War I, Slovenia became one of the six republics of the Socialist Federal Republic of Yugoslavia. Slovenia declared its independence from Yugoslavia in 1991.

People wearing traditional Slovenian costumes

Customs in Slovenia

Slovenia has many fascinating customs and traditions.

- **Carnival plays an important role in Slovenian cluture. The most famous carnival event is the Kurentovanje festival in Ptuj, which takes place in February and includes traditional Kurent masks and costumes.**
- **Easter is an important holiday in Slovenia, with many traditional customs associated with it. Many Slovenians take part in the colouring of Easter eggs, which are decorated with complex designs using natural dyes.**

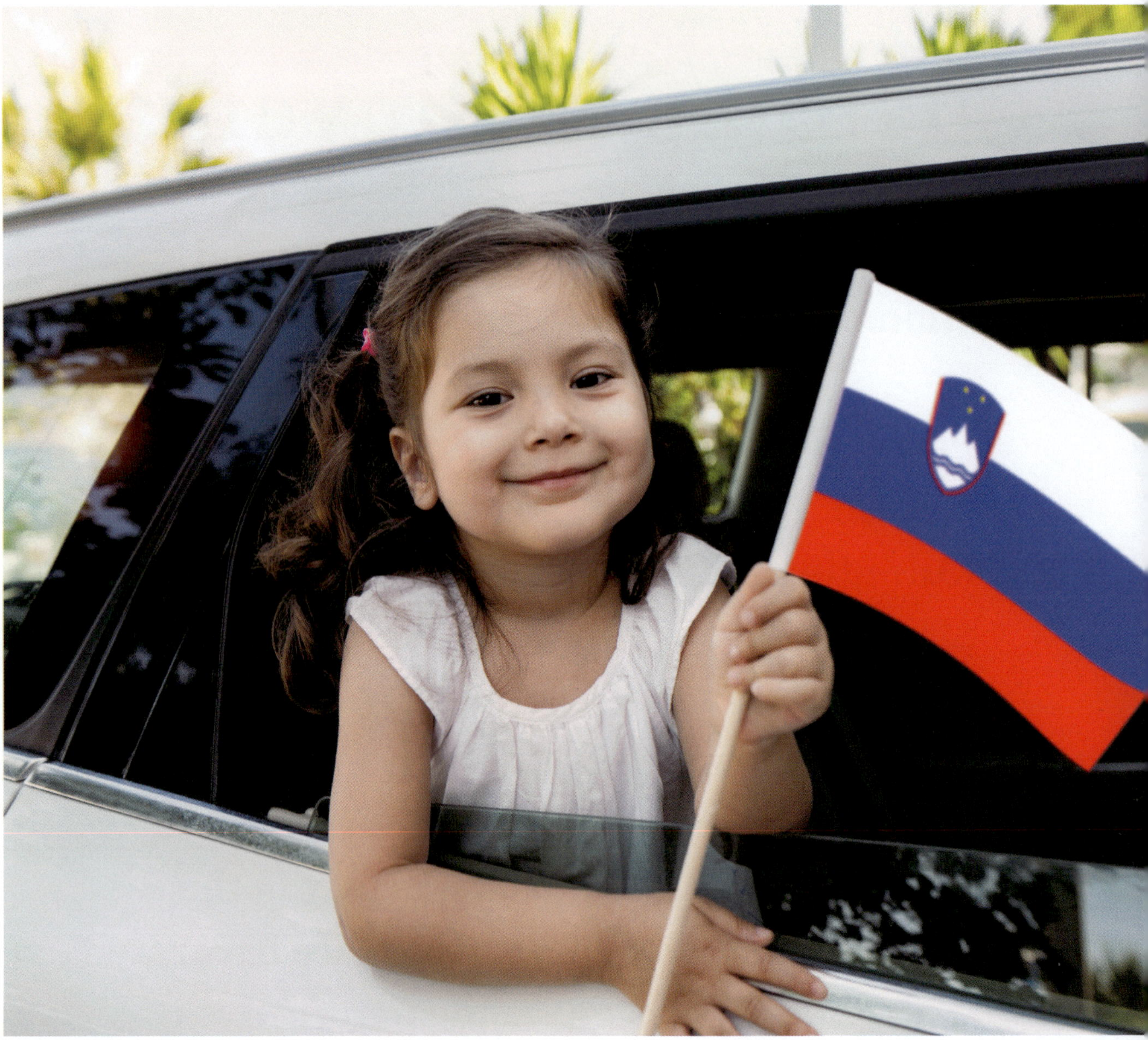

Music of Slovenia

There are many different music genres in Slovenia such as **Folk music, Classical, Pop and Rock.**

Some notable Slovenian musicians include
- **Vlado Kreslin**
- **Lojze Slak**
- **Ansambel Lojzeta Slaka**
- **Laibach**
- **Siddharta**
- **Big Foot Mama**

Ajdovi Žganci Pečenica

Food of Slovenia

Slovenia is known for having delicious, flavoursome and rich dishes.

The national dish of Slovenia is **Ajdovi Žganci Pečenica** which consists of soured turnips and sausages.

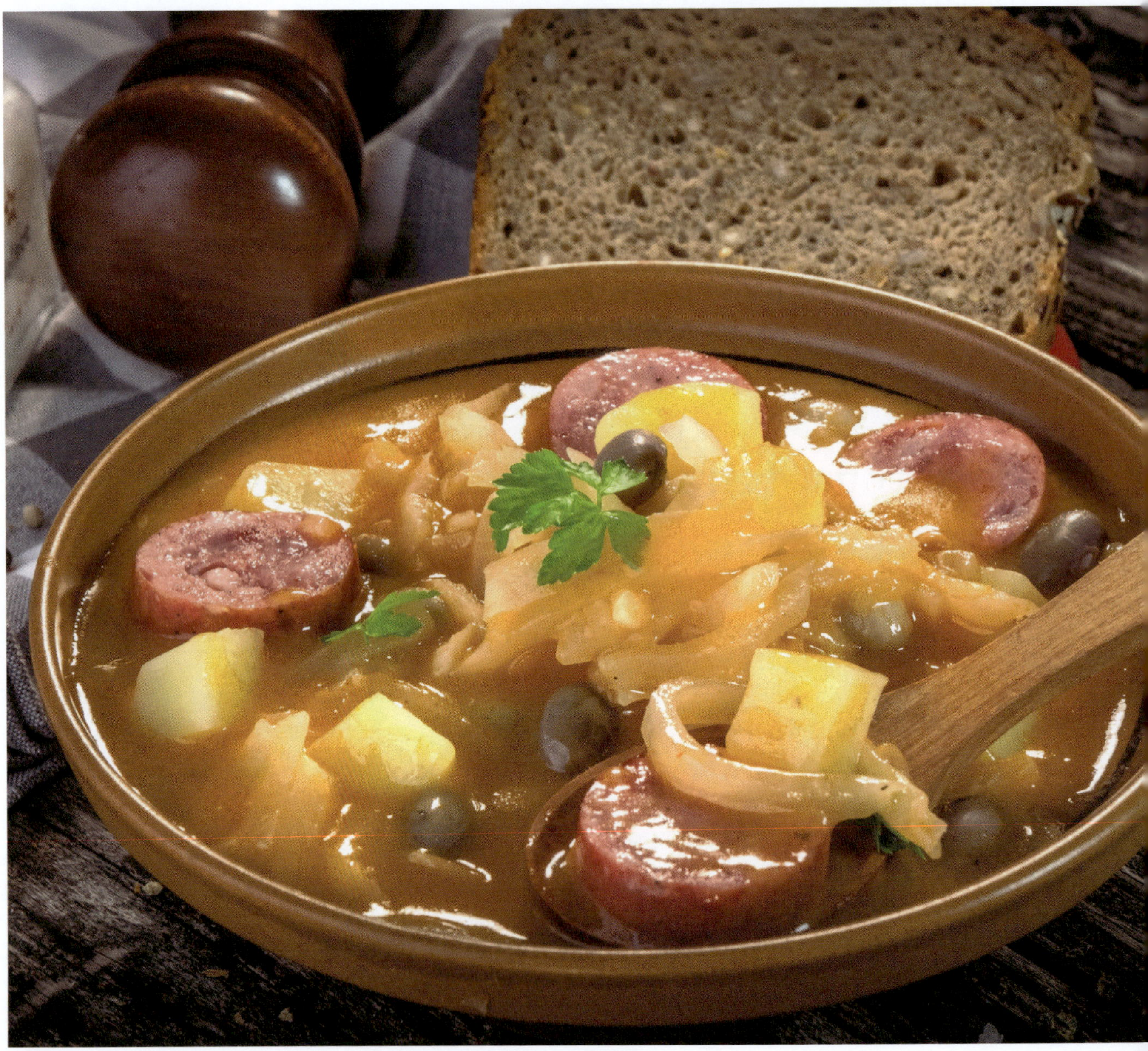

Food of Slovenia

Some popular dishes in Slovenia include

- **Dumplings**
- **Kremna rezina**
- **Kranjska klobasa**
- **Bograč**
- **Idrijski žlikrofi**
- **Pogača**
- **Jota**

Mangart Peak, Slovenia

Weather in Slovenia

Slovenia has a diverse climate due to its location at the crossroads of several climatic zones.

The alpine region of Slovenia has a mountain climate, with cold winters and mild summers and the coastal region of Slovenia has a Mediterranean climate, with mild winters and hot summers.

Young brown bear in Slovenia

Animals of Slovenia

There are many wonderful animals in Slovenia.

Here are some animals that live in Slovenia

- Eurasian lynx
- European wild cats
- Foxes
- European jackal
- Hedgehogs
- Martens
- Snakes

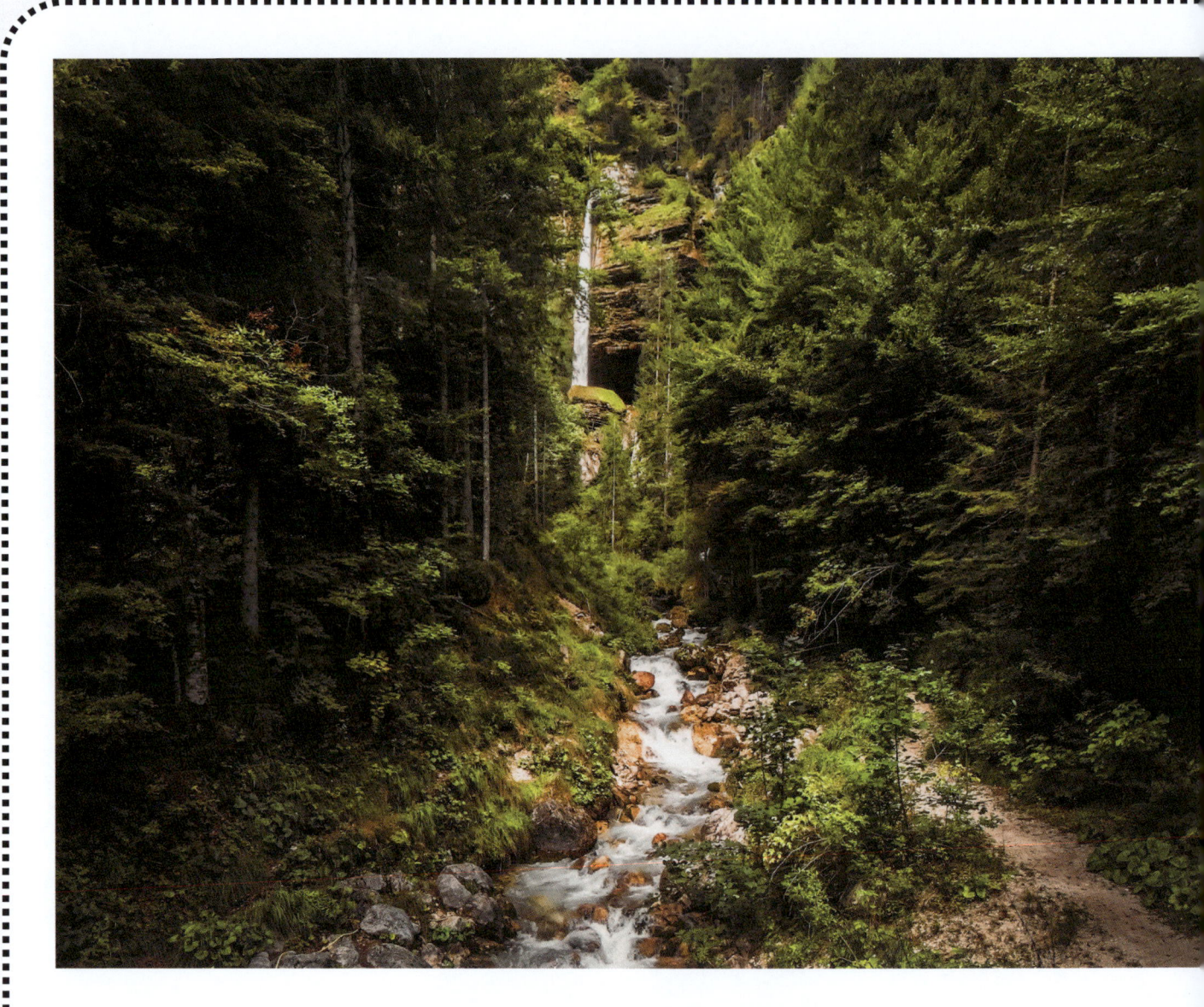

Pericnik Waterfall

Waterfalls

There are many beautiful waterfalls in Slovenia which is one of the reasons why so many people visit this beautiful country every year.

Here are some of Slovenia's waterfalls

- **Pericnik Waterfall**
- **Savica Waterfall**
- **Boka Waterfall**
- **Virje Waterfall**
- **Kozjak Waterfall**
- **Sum Waterfall**

Soccer ball with Slovenian flag

Sports of Slovenia

Sports play an integral part in Slovenian culture. The most popular sport is **Football.**

Here are some of famous sportspeople from Slovenia

- **Janja Garnbret - Rock Climbing**
- **Tina Maze - Skiing**
- **Jolanda Čeplak - Athletics**
- **Tadej Pogačar - Cycling**
- **Anže Kopitar - Hockey**

Slovenian flag

Famous

Many successful people hail from Slovenia.

Here are some notable Slovenian figures

- **Melania Trump – Former First Lady**
- **Goran Dragić – Basketball Player**
- **France Prešeren – Poet**
- **Robert Koren – Footballer**
- **Hugo Wolf - Composer**

People in Piran, Slovenia

Something Extra...

As a little something extra, we are going to share some lesser known facts about Slovenia.

- **Slovenia is home to the oldest vine in the world.**
- **Slovenia is home to one of the largest cave systems in the world called Postojna Cave.**
- **More than half of Slovenia is covered in forests.**

Piran Marina, Slovenia

Words From the Author

We hope that you enjoyed learning about the wonderful country of Slovenia.

Slovenia is a country rich in culture and beauty, with lots of wonderful places to visit and people to meet.

We hope you continue to learn more about this wonderful nation. If you enjoyed this book, consider leaving a review!

With Love

Printed in Dunstable, United Kingdom